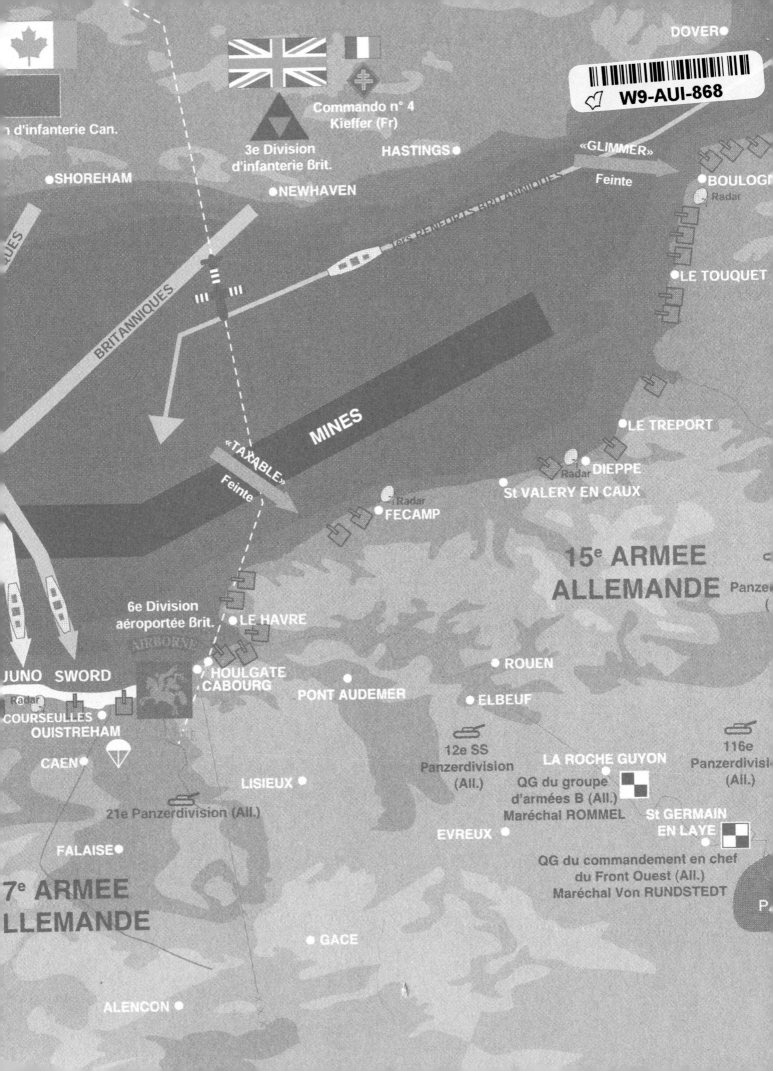

n d'infanterie Can.

DOVER

Commando n° 4
Kieffer (Fr)

3e Division
d'infanterie Brit.

HASTINGS

«GLIMMER»

Feinte

BOULOGI

Radar

SHOREHAM

NEWHAVEN

LE TOUQUET

BRITANNIQUES

LES TRAVERS BRITANNIQUES

LE TREPORT

MINES

«TAXABLE»

Feinte

Radar DIEPPE

St VALERY EN CAUX

Radar

FECAMP

15e ARMEE
ALLEMANDE

Panze

6e Division
aéroportée Brit.

LE HAVRE

AIRBORNE

ROUEN

JUNO   SWORD

HOULGATE
CABOURG

PONT AUDEMER

ELBEUF

Radar

COURSEULLES

OUISTREHAM

LISIEUX

12e SS
Panzerdivision
(All.)

LA ROCHE GUYON

QG du groupe
d'armées B (All.)
Maréchal ROMMEL

116e
Panzerdivis
(All.)

CAEN

21e Panzerdivision (All.)

St GERMAIN
EN LAYE

EVREUX

FALAISE

QG du commandement en chef
du Front Ouest (All.)
Maréchal Von RUNDSTEDT

7e ARMEE
LLEMANDE

GACE

P

ALENCON

NORMANDY

JUNE 44

T. 1 Omaha Beach / Pointe du Hoc

Script : Jean-Blaise DJIAN et Jérôme FELIX
Drawing : Alain PAILLOU
Colours : Catherine MOREAU
Dossier : Isabelle BOURNIER et Marc POTTIER
Translated by : Sylvie LATTONI, Adeline ADAMS
and George KERRICK

EDITIONS
Vagabondages

We would like to thank Pierre-Louis Gosselin
of the BIG RED ONE ASSAULT MUSEUM in
Colleville sur Mer as well as Vincent Hautin for
their technical collaboration
on this comic strip book

Book supported by the Region of Basse Normandie

editionsvagabondages@free.fr
© éditions VAGABONDAGES - DJIAN - FÉLIX - PAILLOU - MOREAU - BOURNIER - POTTIER 2008
First published in France in December 2008
i.s.b.n 9-782918-14304-8
Design : ATELIER 56
Printed in France by CPE Conseil

EUROPE HAD BEEN LIVING HELL UNDER NAZI OPPRESSION FOR NEARLY FIVE YEARS WHEN, ONE APRIL DAY IN LONDON...

YOU DO BEAUTIFUL WORK.

THANKS.

I IMAGINE YOU MUST BE QUITE FAMOUS BACK IN THE STATES.

QUITE THE OPPOSITE, SIR.

MAJOR TREVOR LESTER FROM THE ROYAL ARMY MEDICAL CORPS.

PETER MACTAVISH. SKETCH ARTIST. I VOLUNTEERED FOR THE LANDING.

MAY I ASK YOU A FAVOUR, MR. MACTAVISH?

SURE.

I LIVE IN NEWCASTLE, IN THE NORTH OF ENGLAND, AND GIVEN WHAT'S GOING ON RIGHT NOW, I'M NOT SURE I'LL EVER SEE MY WIFE AGAIN.

IF ANYTHING SHOULD HAPPEN, I WOULD LIKE TO SEND HER A MEMENTO OF US.

I HAVE A PHOTOGRAPH OF HER. COULD YOU DRAW BOTH OF US, CHEEK TO CHEEK, AS IF WE WERE TOGETHER? I WILL PAY ANY PRICE.

1

THIS IS WONDERFUL. YOU ARE A GREAT ARTIST, MR. MACTAVISH.

THANK YOU.

HOW MUCH DO I OWE YOU?

FORGET IT. IT WAS A PLEASURE AND...

GIVEN WHAT AWAITS US, I THINK IT'S BEAUTIFUL TO SEND A LAST MESSAGE TO THE WOMAN YOU LOVE.

THIS IS QUITE EM-BARRASS-ING...

I CANNOT LET YOU GO LIKE THIS. AT LEAST LET ME BUY YOU A BEER.

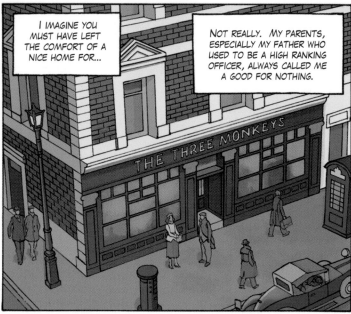

I IMAGINE YOU MUST HAVE LEFT THE COMFORT OF A NICE HOME FOR...

NOT REALLY. MY PARENTS, ESPECIALLY MY FATHER WHO USED TO BE A HIGH RANKING OFFICER, ALWAYS CALLED ME A GOOD FOR NOTHING.

I THOUGHT I COULD MAKE IT IN NEW YORK. I LEFT HOME TO ESCAPE THEIR CRITICISM AND THE CONSTANT COM-PARISON WITH MY BROTHER, JIM, THE SUCCESSFUL ONE.

LAST YEAR, HE EVEN MADE IT INTO THE HEADLINES ACROSS THE COUNTRY...

YOU WERE SAYING YOU WENT TO NEW YORK?

YEAH. AND THERE I MET GLENDA, A SWELL GIRL...

MY PARENTS DON'T APPROVE OF HER AT ALL. SHE GREW UP IN A POOR FAMILY...

2

YOU'RE A NICE CHAP, PETER.

THANKS.

HERE. I WROTE DOWN MY NAME, RANK, ARMY CORPS AND ADDRESS. WHEN THIS CRAZY SHOW IS ALL OVER, YOU'LL ALWAYS BE WELCOME IN MY HOME.

GOOD LUCK!

GOOD LUCK, FRIEND.

THANKS AGAIN.

DEAREST GLENDA,
YOU MUST FORGIVE ME. I'M SORRY, BUT I JUST HAD TO DO IT. PLEASE TRY AND UNDERSTAND. MY FATHER CALLED ME A LOSER AND WAVED THE COVER OF LIFE MAGAZINE IN MY FACE. WHEN I HEARD THE GOVERNMENT WAS LOOKING FOR VOLUNTEERS, I JUST HAD TO ENLIST...

I SHOULD HAVE TOLD YOU. YOU WERE RIGHT TO CHASTISE ME IN YOUR LETTER, BUT I'M BEGGING YOU TO UNDERSTAND MY DECISION. PLEASE DON'T LEAVE ME. YOU ARE THE SUNRISE ON MY HORIZON. I LOVE YOU. PLEASE WAIT FOR ME.
YOUR PETER

MAY 8TH, 1944, IN LONDON. GENERAL MONTGOMERY REPORTED THAT THE ALLIED TROOPS HAD REACHED THEIR HEIGHT OF READINESS. IT WAS TIME TO SET THE DATE FOR THE LANDING OPERATION. THEY CHOSE THE 5TH OF JUNE AT DAWN.

ON MAY 15TH, BEFORE THE KING OF ENGLAND AND SIR WINSTON CHURCHILL, AIR MARSHAL A.W. TEDDER PRESENTED THE FINAL PLANS TO THE ALLIED HIGH COMMAND. THE LANDING WOULD TAKE PLACE IN NORMANDY BETWEEN THE MOUTH OF THE RIVER ORNE AND CARENTAN BAY.

US TROOPS WILL LAND ON UTAH AND OMAHA WHILE BRITISH AND CANADIAN FORCES WILL LAND ON GOLD, JUNO, AND SWORD BEACHES.

IN PREPARATION, AIRBORNE FORCES WILL PARACHUTE TO THE WEST OF CARENTAN BAY AND TO THE EAST OF THE ORNE.

TWO WEEKS BEFORE D-DAY, MORE THAN 1.5 MILLION SOLDIERS WERE LOCKED UP IN CAMPS CALLED 'SAUSAGE CAMPS.' IT WAS THERE THE MEN LEARNED THAT THE LANDING WOULD TAKE PLACE IN NORMANDY.

OPERATION FORTITUDE WAS A DECOY OPERATION TO SPREAD THE IDEA THAT THE LANDINGS WOULD TAKE PLACE IN THE PAS DE CALAIS.

WITH THIS NEW KNOWLEDGE, NO ONE WAS ALLOWED TO LEAVE CAMP. THE GUARDS, WHO WERE NOT IN THE KNOW, HAD ORDERS TO FIRE UPON ANYONE TRYING TO VIOLATE THIS ORDER.

INSIDE CAMP WEYMOUTH, THE MOOD WAS HEAVY AND TENSE. EVERYBODY KNEW THAT TRAINING, WHICH FOR SOME HAD BEEN GOING ON FOR YEARS, WAS OVER. MANY MEN WOULD LOSE THEIR LIVES.

GLENDA DARLING, YOU HAVEN'T ANSWERED MY LAST LETTER. I THINK OF YOU ALWAYS. THE DAY OF DAYS IS APPROACHING. THIS LETTER WON'T BE SENT UNTIL AFTER THE LANDING, BUT I WANTED YOU TO KNOW HOW MUCH I LOVE YOU...

MY SKETCHES WILL BECOME PROPAGANDA POSTERS AND WILL SURELY BE PUBLISHED IN MAGAZINES. I HOPE MY FATHER WILL BE PROUD OF ME FOR ONCE.

YOU WILL SEE THAT EVERYTHING IS GOING TO BE JUST SWELL FOR US. I WANTED TO KEEP IT A SURPRISE, BUT MR. SPENCER PROMISED TO HIRE ME AT HIS ADVERTISING AGENCY WITH A GOOD SALARY WHEN I GET BACK.

HERE, SERGEANT.

ANOTHER ONE! I TOLD YOU MACTAVISH; YOUR LETTERS WON'T BE SENT UNTIL AFTER THE OPERATION...

??!

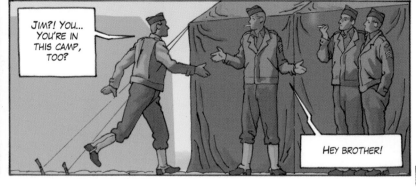

JIM?! YOU... YOU'RE IN THIS CAMP, TOO?

HEY BROTHER!

4

6

I HEARD THAT YOU'D VOLUNTEERED WHEN I WAS HOME IN MARCH. I HOPE YOU REALLY THOUGHT THROUGH THIS THING. IT'S GOING TO BE A BLOODY BATTLE...

COME ON. LET'S GO GET A COLD BEER.

YOU'RE NOT CUT OUT FOR THIS...

SO, YOU'RE GONNA BE LIKE ROBERT CAPA BUT WITH A CHARCOAL PENCIL? WHAT UNIT ARE YOU WITH?

I'LL BE WITH THE 1ST DIVISION, 5TH ARMY CORPS.

AND YOU?

THE FAMOUS BIG RED ONE!

THEY'RE THE ONES THAT FOUGHT IN NORTH AFRICA AND SICILY... THEIR OBJECTIVE IS OMAHA BEACH, RIGHT?

I'M WITH THE 2ND BATTALION OF THE RANGERS. WE'VE BEEN TRAINING FOR TWO YEARS NOW. OUR TARGET IS GONNA BE THE CLIFF AT POINTE DU HOC. WE HAVE TO PREVENT ANY ATTACK ON OUR SHIPS BY NEUTRALIZING THE SIX BIG CANNONS AT THE TOP.

HOW HAVE THE FOLKS BEEN?

THEY'RE DOING ALL RIGHT, BUT I WASN'T REALLY AT HOME... I HAD TO DO SOME STUFF IN NEW YORK...

OH YEAH? LIKE WHAT?

THE NEWSPAPERS WROTE ABOUT ME LAST YEAR. I'VE BECOME SOME SORT OF SYMBOL FOR OUR TROOPS. THOUSANDS OF READERS HAD WRITTEN TO ME FOR AN UPDATE...

SO I WENT THERE...DID A FEW PRESS CONFERENCES... TO RAISE THE MORALE OF THE SOLDIERS' FAMILIES, YOU KNOW.

5

ON JUNE 2ND, SEVERAL PLANES TOOK OFF FROM THE THORNEY ISLAND AIRFIELD.

THEIR MISSION: NEUTRALIZE GERMAN RADAR AND RADIO STATIONS.

THE ATTACKS AND BROADCASTS BY RADIO LONDON ALLOWED THE GERMANS TO KNOW THAT D-DAY WAS COMING SOON.

FIELD MARSHAL ROMMEL, GREAT STRATEGIST AND MASTERMIND BEHIND THE "ATLANTIC WALL," WARNED HIS OFFICERS...

IF YOU THINK THEY'LL ARRIVE IN NICE WEATHER, TAKING THE SHORTEST WAY AND WARNING YOU IN ADVANCE, YOU'RE ALL WRONG! THE ALLIES WILL LAND IN AWFUL WEATHER, CHOOSING THE LONGEST ROUTE...

THEY'LL LAND HERE, IN NORMANDY.

INDEED, ON THE NIGHT OF THE 4TH AND 5TH OF JUNE, A FORMIDABLE ARMADA LEFT THE ENGLISH COASTS IN AWFUL WEATHER.

ALREADY THIS BAD AT 0400 HOURS...

TEDDER, OUR MEN CANNOT LAND TOMORROW. D-DAY IS GOING TO BE DELAYED ONE FULL DAY... IF THE WEATHER IMPROVES, THAT IS.

ALL CONVOYS ALREADY AT SEA MUST RETURN TO PORT.

128 SHIPS WOULD NOT RECEIVE THIS ORDER. A FLYING BOAT WAS SENT TO ORDER THEIR RETURN.

6

WEATHER SPECIALISTS ANNOUNCED A BREAK IN THE WEATHER ON THE 5TH OF JUNE. IN THE SOUTHWICK HOUSE LIBRARY, THE SUPREME HEADQUARTERS ALLIED EXPEDITIONARY FORCE DECIDED TO LAUNCH OPERATION OVERLORD THE NEXT MORNING.

AT THE NORTH WITHAM AND GREENHAM COMMON AIR FORCE BASES, AS AT ALL THE OTHERS, ANXIETY MOUNTED WHEN THE 940 PLANES TOOK OFF.

ACCORDING TO THE ORIGINAL PLAN, THE 101ST AIRBORNE DIVISION, "THE SCREAMING EAGLES," LED BY GENERAL M TAYLOR JUMPED ABOVE CARENTAN BAY TO FACILITATE THE LANDING ON UTAH BEACH.

THIS TIME AROUND, THE MACHINE WAS EN ROUTE. THERE WAS NO TURNING BACK.

MEANWHILE, CROSSING THE CHANNEL, ADMIRAL BERTRAM RAMSAY, WHO HAD ALREADY LED THE OPERATION TORCH LANDINGS, WAS LEADING A FLEET OF 6,000 SHIPS.

7

9

SIR TRAFFORD LEIGH-MALLORY, APPOINTED AIR COMMANDER-IN-CHIEF, WAS ASSIGNED TO BOMB THE FRENCH COASTS, INCLUDING THOSE IN THE PAS DE CALAIS TO CONTINUE DECEIVING THE GERMANS.

AT THE MOUTH OF THE ORNE AND WITH GREAT ACCURACY, THREE HORSA GLIDERS FLEW IN ABOUT 90 MEN FROM THE BRITISH 6TH AIRBORNE DIVISION UNDER THE COMMAND OF MAJOR HOWARD. THEIR EMBLEM WAS PEGASUS.

TWO OTHER GLIDERS LANDED SUCCESSFULLY NEAR THE RANVILLE BRIDGE; THE THIRD WAS LOST. THE GOAL OF THEIR OPERATION: CAPTURE AND HOLD TWO BRIDGES INTACT UNTIL RELIEVED. THE BRITISH WOULD ACHIEVE THIS AFTER ONLY 15 MINUTES AND AT THE PRICE OF 2 KILLED AND 14 INJURED SOLDIERS.

ON THE COTENTIN PENINSULA, OPERATIONS PROVED FAR MORE DIFFICULT; 2,499 SOLDIERS WERE EITHER SHOT DOWN BY THE ENEMY OR DROWNED IN THE MARSHES.

IN HIS LANDING CRAFT, PETER WAS LIVID. THE STORM WAS NOT CALMING. EXHAUSTED BY 24 HOURS WITHOUT SLEEP AND DRUGGED BY DRAMAMINE, THE SOLDIERS WERE IN BAD SHAPE.

LOST IN MEMORIES THAT COULD VERY WELL BE THEIR LAST, THE SOLDIERS WERE STOIC AND SILENT AS BOMBS FROM THE PLANES EXPLODED IN THE DISTANCE.

8

AROUND 0300 HOURS, THE SHIPS CARRYING THE 2ND BATTALION OF US RANGERS, LED BY COLONEL RUDDER, STOPPED THEIR ENGINES AT 12 NAUTICAL MILES FROM THE POINTE DU HOC.

WHY ARE WE STOPPING SO FAR OUT, CAPTAIN?

THEIR GPFS* HAVE A MAXIMUM RANGE OF 13 MILES. THEY'LL NEVER BE ABLE TO REACH US IN THIS WEATHER**.

THE SEA IS ROUGH. IT'LL TAKE HOURS FOR THE BOATS TO REACH THE COAST.

BETWEEN TWO OR THREE... IN THE MEAN TIME, THE 14-INCH CANNONS WILL COVER THEM.

BAOOM

THE THREE COMPANIES*** OF THE FIRST ASSAULT WAVE WERE ACCOMPANIED BY TWO LCAs**** CARRYING FOOD, MEDICINE, AND AMMUNITION.

YOU DON'T LOOK GOOD, JIM. FUNNY SEEING AS YOU'VE ALREADY PROVEN TO BE SO COURAGEOUS. LIKE THAT TIME WHEN...

IT'S PETER! MY BROTHER... HE VOLUNTEERED FOR THE LANDING AT OMAHA WITH THE BIG RED ONE.

SO? AND YOU'RE NOT LANDING?

FOR ME, IT'S MY JOB. BUT HIM... HE'S AN ARTIST, A DAYDREAMER. JUST CANNON FODDER...

*155MM CANNON OF FRENCH ORIGIN. **A 4 OR 5 ON THE BEAUFORT WIND FORCE SCALE. *** FOX, DOG, AND EASY. **** BRITISH LANDING CRAFT.

9

SERGEANT! WATER!...
WE'RE TAKING ON WATER!

USE YOUR HELMETS!
SCOOP IT OUT!

HO!

WHAT IS IT,
CAPTAIN?

WE'VE GOT A PROBLEM. THOSE DAMNED
WOODEN LCAS ARE TAKING ON WATER!

WE'RE NOT GONNA MAKE IT, CAPTAIN!

IT'S COMIN' IN TOO FAST.
WE'RE GONNA SINK!

ALREADY LOST TWO
BOATS AND WE'RE
TAKING ON WATER TOO!

START SCOOPIN',
BURKIN!

WHAT SHALL WE
DO, CAPTAIN?

NOTHING. AN LCA
WILL FISH THEM OUT ON
THE WAY BACK.

MEANWHILE, NEAR OMAHA BEACH..

A GREAT ARTIST ONCE TOLD ME THAT IF MY DRAWINGS ARE BAD, IT'S BECAUSE I'M NOT CLOSE ENOUGH TO THE MODEL.

TODAY, I'M GONNA BE IN THE HEART OF THE ACTION.

SO IF MY SKETCHES AREN'T ANY GOOD THIS TIME AROUND, EVERYONE WHO DIDN'T BELIEVE IN ME WILL HAVE BEEN RIGHT.

AFTER SICILY AND NORTH AFRICA, LIKE MY BROTHER SAID, NOBODY IN THE BIG RED ONE HAS ANYTHING LEFT TO PROVE.

AND YET, FEW OF THEM ASKED TO GO HOME. I WONDER WHY?

WHAT'S DRIVING THEM INTO COMBAT AGAIN? ME... I'VE GOT NOTHING TO LOSE.

BUT THEM?

THEY RESPECT EACH OTHER...

...RELY ON ONE ANOTHER.

THEY IGNORE ME...

WHO CAN BLAME 'EM ?

THEY SENT ME, A DOODLER, EVEN THOUGH DOCTORS WEREN'T ALLOWED TO PARTICIPATE IN THE FIRST WAVE SO AS TO HAVE AS MANY FIGHTERS AS POSSIBLE. I DRAW...

HEUU...

11

13

BLAAAHHH!

HEY! DO YOU HAVE ANY EXTRA BENZEDRINE ? I LOST MINE.

DON'T TAKE THAT SHIT! IT'LL MAKE YOU DIZZY.

BETTER TO ARRIVE FRESH WHERE WE'RE HEADED... BELIEVE ME.

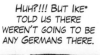

HUH?!!! BUT IKE* TOLD US THERE WEREN'T GOING TO BE ANY GERMANS THERE.

SURE, AND THERE ARE GORGEOUS FRENCH GIRLS WAITING FOR US ON THE BEACH.

BUT INTELLIGENCE** WAS POSITIVE: THE GERMANS GUARDING THIS BEACH WERE EITHER TOO YOUNG, TOO OLD, OR TOO INJURED TO FIGHT ON THE EASTERN FRONT.

THEY'RE PREDOMINANTLY POLISH AND RUSSIAN DRAFTEES GUARDING THIS BEACH.

THESE GUYS WERE BROUGHT HERE AGAINST THEIR WILL. DO YOU REALLY THINK THEY WOULD HAVE STAYED IN THEIR BUNKERS, WAITING TO GET KILLED ?

I DON'T KNOW, BUT ONE THING'S FOR SURE...

...THIS SILENCE IS THAT OF SEASONED SOLDIERS.

THREE DAYS BEFORE D-DAY, THE 3RD REGIMENT, COMPOSED OF EXPERIENCED SOLDIERS RETURNING FROM THE EASTERN FRONT, JOINED THE FORCES ALREADY GUARDING THE COAST.

DON'T SHOOT. WAIT FOR THE RAMPS TO COME DOWN. THE GIS WILL PANIC AND JUMP IN THE WATER.

LIKE LAMBS TO THE SLAUGHTER!

ON LAND, THE CANNONS RECEIVED ORDERS TO FIRE.

* EISENHOWER: SUPREME COMMANDER OF THE ALLIED EXPEDITIONARY FORCE IN EUROPE. ** A SECRET INTELLIGENCE SERVICE

ALL RIGHT... HERE WE GO!

LORD, I'M GONNA BE REAL BUSY. PROBABLY WON'T HAVE ENOUGH TIME TO THINK ABOUT YOU. PLEASE DON'T FORGET ABOUT ME.

HE'S TERRIFIED. TO THINK THAT HE COULD BE AT HOME WITH HIS GIRLFRIEND!

WHY DIDN'T YOU GO BACK HOME?

YOU COULDN'T UNDERSTAND!

WHY'S THAT?

ROCKET!!!

THANK GOD.

LOOK. WHOLE COAST IS COVERED IN FOG!

THE WIND MUST HAVE BLOWN BACK THE SMOKE FROM THE BOMBINGS AND THE GERMAN CANNONS.

ONCE WE'RE ON THE BEACH, WE WON'T SEE A THING. NOT EVEN WHERE THE GERMANS ARE SHOOTING FROM.

THE MEN ARE PANICKING, SERGEANT.

THEY'RE GONNA LOSE IT. YOU GOTTA REASSURE 'EM.

LISTEN UP ONE LAST TIME!

THE AMPHIBIOUS TANKS WERE PUT INTO WATER 4 HOURS AGO.

WHEN WE LAND...

...THEY'LL ALREADY BE ON THE BEACH, READY TO COVER US.

TAKE COVER BEHIND 'EM OR DIVE INTO THE SHELL CRATERS FROM EARLIER BOMBINGS. AND BELIEVE ME, THE HOLES...

...THERE'LL BE PLENTY OF 'EM...PLENTY OF 'EM...

...EVERYWHERE !

THEN RUN UP TO THE ANTI-TANK WALL AND BLOW IT TO GAIN ACCESS TO THE VALLEY. WITHOUT IT, THE VEHICLES IN THE SECOND WAVE WON'T BE ABLE TO ADVANCE INLAND.

WE'VE GOT 30 MINUTES TO DO OUR JOB. I WANT A CLEAR PATH WHEN THIS DAMNED SECOND ASSAULT WAVE HITS !

GET READY TO GO !

ARE YOU BLIND ?

WE'RE STILL ANOTHER 200 YARDS FROM THE BEACH!

THERE ARE TOO MANY SANDBARS. I CAN'T RISK GETTING STUCK IN THE SAND.

AND WITHOUT THE LCVPS, WE WON'T HAVE ANY REINFORCEMENTS.

GO!

14

16

AND JUST LIKE THAT, THE LCVP RAMPS CAME CRASHING DOWN INTO THE ICY WATER...

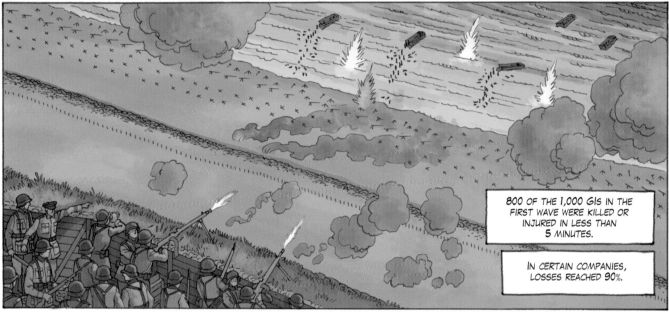

800 OF THE 1,000 GIs IN THE FIRST WAVE WERE KILLED OR INJURED IN LESS THAN 5 MINUTES.

IN CERTAIN COMPANIES, LOSSES REACHED 90%.

JUMP OVERBOARD!

YOUR TURN, DOODLER!

GET A MOVE ON!

HE'S TOO HEAVY! HIS ASSAULT JACKET IS DRAGGING HIM TO THE BOTTOM.

THANK GOD THEY WEREN'T ISSUED TO ARTISTS.

OPEN UP GOD DAMN IT.

COME ON!

DAMN...

15

SPREAD OUT! DON'T STAY TOGETHER!!!

TAKE OFF YOUR JACKETS, FELLAS! FORGET ABOUT THE GEAR.

I CAN'T!

CAN'T UNDO THESE DAMNED STRAPS!

THEY'RE TOTALLY SWOLLEN. THE STRAPS ARE TOO WET.

BECAUSE OF THE WATER SATURATION, THE 130 POUNDS OF GEAR THAT THE GIS WERE CARRYING WEIGHED MORE LIKE 220.

THEY LOOK LIKE TURTLES!

COMPLETELY EXHAUSTED, ONLY A FEW SURVIVORS REACHED THE BEACH.

SOME LITERALLY COLLAPSED FROM EXHAUSTION.

MANY WOULD NEVER GET BACK UP.

16

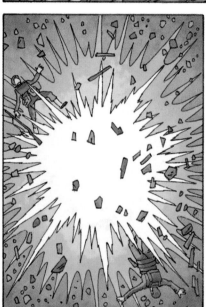

?!!!

WHERE ARE THE OTHER TANKS?

AT THE BOTTOM OF THE SEA...

ALMOST ALL OF THEM SANK.

HOW ? HADN'T THEY BEEN TESTED?

YEAH, ON LAKES... NOT ON A SQUALLY SEA. THE FLOTATION DEVICES GAVE UP IN LESS THAN 5 MINUTES.

HEY!

WHERE'S THE ANTI-TANK WALL WE'RE S'POSED TO DESTROY.

DAMN IT! WE WEREN'T DEPLOYED IN THE RIGHT SPOT!

WHAT SHALL WE DO?

MORTAR FIRE!!!

THE KRAUTS ARE GONNA BLOW THESE ROCKS EVERYWHERE!!!

TAKE COVER!

AT THAT MOMENT, OUR SOLE PROTECTION BECAME OUR WORST ENEMY.

19

21

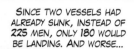

NEAR THE POINTE DU HOC...

...THE LCAs WERE TAKING ON WATER, SOAKING EQUIPMENT, BUT THAT WASN'T WHAT WORRIED RUDDER THE MOST...

SINCE TWO VESSELS HAD ALREADY SUNK, INSTEAD OF 225 MEN, ONLY 180 WOULD BE LANDING. AND WORSE...

TURN BACK! THE LEAD COXSWAIN MADE A MISTAKE ! WE'RE NOT HEADED TOWARD THE POINTE DU HOC. THE CURRENTS ARE TAKING US TOO FAR EAST !

WHAT A DISASTER ! THE ATTACK PLAN IS ALL MESSED UP.

INSTEAD OF HAVING TWO COMPANIES LANDING ON ONE SIDE OF THE CLIFF AND THE THIRD ON THE OTHER, WE'RE ALL GONNA LAND ON THE EAST SIDE.

WITH THIS DELAY, WE'RE NOT GONNA BE ABLE TO TAKE THE CLIFF BY 0700 HOURS. THEY WON'T SEND REINFORCEMENTS UNTIL WE CAN LIGHT UP THAT FLARE.

0710 HOURS

200 GERMAN GUNNERS WERE THERE TO WELCOME THE US RANGERS. DESPITE THEIR SKILL, AND EXHAUSTED FROM A SLEEPLESS NIGHT, THE MEN WERE OVERWHELMED.

RUDDER STILL HASN'T SET OFF THE FLARE. THE OPERATION IS A FIASCO! WE'RE GONNA HAVE TO SEND IN THE 500 RANGERS WHO WERE SUPPOSED TO HELP OUT AT OMAHA.

THE "POTATO SMASHER" GRENADES, ROCKS, AND GERMAN FIRE QUICKLY KILLED 15 RANGERS.

GOD DAMN!

WHAT'S GOING ON NOW?

MOST OF THE GRAPNEL ROCKETS ARE SOAKED, SARGE! THE ROPES ARE TOO HEAVY TO REACH THE TOP OF THE CLIFF.

FIRE THE ONES THAT WORK! WE DON'T HAVE THE CHOICE. GOTTA ADAPT!

IT'S GETTING WORSE, COLONEL. WE'VE ALREADY LOST TWENTY MEN...

THE DUKWS* ARE ARRIVING. THEY'LL HELP US OUT...

* DUKWS: AN AMERICAN AMPHIBIOUS TRUCK DESIGNED BY GMC, FIXED WITH A BORROWED LADDER FROM THE LONDON FIRE DEPARTMENT. AT THE TOP OF THE LADDER WAS A BRITISH DOUBLE MACHINE-GUN.

THE GERMAN SOLDIERS FOUND IT DIFFICULT TO FALL BACK SINCE THE GROUND ATOP THE CLIFF HAD BEEN SO HEAVILY BOMBED.

THEY'RE ATTACKING FROM THE TRENCHES.

FIVE MINUTES HERE, THEN THEY'LL DISAPPEAR AND REAPPEAR WHERE WE WON'T HEAR THEM...

THIS COULD GET ROUGH... HANG IN THERE, FELLAS!

RUDDER HERE. THE HOC IS ALMOST SECURED... HEAVY LOSSES... NEED REINFORCEMENTS IMMEDIATELY...

GOOD WORK... NEGATIVE ON THE REINFORCEMENTS. THEY'RE ALREADY AT OMAHA.

22

ONE HOUR LATER...

HEY!

WHAT IS IT, SERGEANT?

WE LOST ABOUT 60 MEN* FOR NOTHING. LOOK, CAPTAIN.

OUT OF THE SIX FAMOUS CANNONS AT POINTE DU HOC THAT WE WERE SUPPOSED TO DESTROY, FIVE OF THEM ARE DAMNED TELEPHONE POLES! AND THE OTHER ONE** WAS ALREADY TAKEN CARE OF...

WE TRAINED TO CLIMB CLIFFS FOR THE LAST SIX MONTHS FOR TELEPHONE POLES! WE CLIMBED UP THIS THING FOR NOTHING!

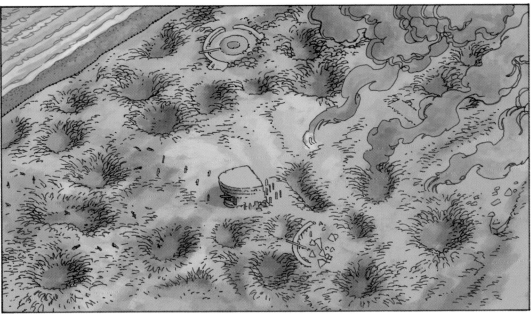

IT'S A 22 MILLIMETRE CANNON...

WE'D BETTER GET GOING ON OUR SECOND MISSION : TAKE CONTROL OF THE COASTAL HIGHWAY AND THE INTERSECTION TO KEEP THE GERMANS FROM SENDING REINFORCEMENTS TO OMAHA BEACH !

* TWO-THIRDS INJURED, ONE-THIRD DEAD.   **THIS CANNON HAD BEEN DESTROYED IN A BOMBING TWO WEEKS EARLIER.

25

 DURING THIS TIME ON OMAHA BEACH...

HELP! HE.. HELP ME.

 WE'RE ALL GONNA DIE !

STAY STRONG. THE SECOND ASSAULT WAVE 'S GONNA BE HERE IN 20 MINUTES !

 STRANGELY, IT WAS IN THE MIDDLE OF THIS HELL THAT I REMEMBERED WHY I WAS THERE.

 ALL AROUND ME, THE ZEAL FOR COMBAT HAD BEEN REPLACED BY A STATE OF LIFELESSNESS.

 NOBODY MOVED A MUSCLE.

AND SOME WHO HAD TAKEN TOO MUCH DRAMAMINE EVEN FELL ASLEEP.

 EVERYBODY WAS TENSE, EDGY...

I HELD ON TO MY DRAWING.

 SUDDENLY, AND IN A STATE OF TOTAL MADNESS*, SOME GIS BEGAN GETTING UP AND WALKING AROUND IN A TRANCE AS IF NOTHING WAS HAPPENING. THESE MEN BECAME EASY TARGETS.

 MEANWHILE, THE TIDE WAS COMING IN.

 KI... KILL ME !

DON'T LET ME DIE LIKE THIS !

IF ONLY HE KNEW THAT I DON'T EVEN HAVE A GUN !...

*SEVERAL SOLDIERS ON THE BEACH SUFFERED FROM HALLUCINATIONS; FIRING IN EVERY DIRECTION AROUND THEM, INCLUDING AT THEIR FELLOW SOLDIERS.

EVERYTHING AROUND ME WAS EXPLODING. I FELT LIKE I WAS HIDING BEHIND MY SKETCHPAD AND PENCILS...

NO!

?!!!

REINFORCEMENTS ARE HERE!

THE SECOND ASSAULT WAVE ARRIVED AS PLANNED 30 MINUTES AFTER THE FIRST. AND UNFORTUNATELY, THE TIDE HAD COME IN JUST ENOUGH TO COVER THE BEACH'S OBSTACLES.

BAOUM

BY CHANCE, SOME LCVPs MANAGED TO MAKE IT THROUGH THE MINES.

BUT SINCE NOBODY TOLD THE GIS TO TAKE OFF THEIR ASSAULT JACKETS...

...THE SECOND WAVE PASSED MUCH LIKE THE FIRST.

...AN ABSOLUTE DISASTER.

THE FEW SURVIVORS SCATTERED THEMSELVES OUT ALL ALONG THE BEACH, EXACTLY LIKE THE FIRST WAVE HAD DONE ONLY **30** MINUTES EARLIER.

I'VE GOT THE BANGALORE*!

SOMEBODY KNOW HOW TO USE THESE THINGS?

OVER HERE!

YOU A COMBAT ENGINEER, SERGEANT?

NO, BUT I'VE USED THIS KIND OF THING ALREADY IN SICILY.

TAKE COVER!

IT'S GONNA BLOW!

*THE BANGALORE TORPEDO WAS AN EXPLOSIVE DEVICE USED TO DEMOLISH BARBED WIRE FENCING.

26

BAOUM

SERGEANT, THE GERMANS ARE SNIPING US FROM THE BUNKERS OVER ON THE LEFT.

BUT IF WE CAN MAKE IT TO THE BOTTOM OF THAT HILL, WE'LL BE OUT OF THEIR FIELD OF VISION.

RUN ALL THE WAY TO THE CLIFF, SERGEANT?

THERE'S NO COVER. IT'S WIDE OPEN!

THE KRAUTS'LL SHOOT AT US LIKE WE'RE RABBITS.

TWO KINDS OF PEOPLE ARE GOING TO STAY ON THIS BEACH...

I'M SAYIN' WE'VE GOTTA TRY OUR LUCK.

THE VILLA IN RUINS! HE MADE IT!

THAT'S MORE THAN HALF THE WAY THERE.

TATATATA

THE DEAD AND THOSE WHO ARE ABOUT TO DIE.

GET ALL THE BOYS TOGETHER. WE'VE GOTTA JOIN HIM!

AT 0710 HOURS, 23 GIS MADE A RUN FOR IT IN AN OPERATION INSPIRED BY UTTER DESPERATION.

29

BARELY HALF OF THE MEN WOULD REACH THE VILLA IN RUINS.

CAREFUL BOYS. LOOKS LIKE THERE'S A MINE FIELD BETWEEN US AND THAT CLIFF.

IF THE GERMANS MINED THIS AREA, SARGE...

IT'S 'CAUSE THEY KNOW THIS POSITION IS VULNERABLE. WE'VE GOTTA GIVE IT A GO.

THIS TIME, I'M GOING FIRST!

OK. FIND US A PASSAGEWAY.

TAKE COVER IN THE GRASS! THE KRAUTS WON'T BE ABLE TO KEEP YOU IN THEIR SIGHTS!

ATATATA

PLAOUF

SLOW AND STEADY.

WELL... NOT THAT WAY.

HUH???

THE GRASS IS PARTED 'CAUSE SOMEONE AL-READY CAME THROUGH!

THERE'S A TRAIL!

GOD IS WITH US, BOYS! GO!

28

30

CRAWLING FOR THEIR LIVES, THE 13 REMAINING GIS MADE IT TO THE BASE OF THE CLIFF UNSCATHED.

NOW WE SHOULD BE ABLE TO CLIMB UP THERE WITHOUT A PROBLEM.

STAY IN SINGLE FILE AND MOVE QUICKLY!

WAIT A MOMENT LONGER... THERE...

FIRE!

TA TA TATA

BATTLE-HARDENED BY COMBAT IN SICILY AND NORTH AFRICA, THE SERGEANT DOES NOT PANIC...

SMOKE GRENADES! SPREAD OUT!

ATTACK FROM ALL SIDES!

THERE!

AND THERE!

31

THERE'S ONE LEFT!

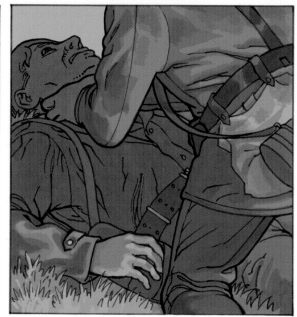

OH NO!

CRAC

BLAM

WHERE DO YOU THINK YOU ARE?

NONE OF US WANTED THIS WAR, BUT WE'RE HERE FIGHTING!

EVERY GUY OUT HERE WAS BROUGHT UP BY THEIR PARENTS TO BE NICE BOYS.

TOM WAS A FLORIST. HERBERT WAS A BAKER...

NOTHING BUT A BUNCH OF WILLING GUYS WHO WERE THROWN INTO COMBAT AND ASKED TO BECOME PROFESSIONAL KILLERS. AND THAT'S EXACTLY WHAT THEY ARE NOW!

SO IF YOU WANT TO SURVIVE IN THIS HELL, GRAB A GUN...

...AND USE IT.

IF NOT... JUST STAY HERE...

... AND HIDE!!

OH NO!

GERMANS ARE GOING TO AMBUSH THEM!

THEY'LL BE SLAUGHTERED...

33

THEY DIDN'T SEE US.

KEEP QUIET.

FIRE!

TAKATAKATAKATA

?!?

BUT?!!! THAT'S THE DOODLER!

THE AMERICANS ARE APPROACHING!

TAKE NO PRISONERS!

IF WE CAN TAKE THIS MACHINE GUN NEST, WE'LL FREE UP A LANDING ON THE BEACH. WITHOUT IT, OUR GUYS WILL BE STUCK OUT ON THE EMBANKMENT, TRAPPED BY ENEMY FIRE!

ATTACK!!!

BY GRENADES,

GUNS,

OR HAND-TO-HAND COMBAT,

WE ATTACKED THE GERMANS...

I LIKE ALL THE OTHERS.

AT THAT SAME MOMENT, THE SITUATION HAD BECOME CRITICAL.

HURRY AND BLOW UP THESE GOD DAMNED HEDGEHOGS!

THEY'RE GONNA BLOW!

GET AWAY FROM THE HEDGEHOGS! THE ENGINEERS ARE GONNA SET 'EM OFF! GET OUT OF THE WAY!

WHILE WAITING FOR THE ENGINEERS TO FINALLY CLEAR OFF PARTS OF THE BEACH, THE MAJOR GENERAL GAVE THE ORDER TO STOP DEBARKING ALL VEHICLES.

THIS LEFT ABOUT TWENTY TRANSPORTERS CIRCLING IN THE CHANNEL. WITH LITTLE FUEL, THE VESSELS WOULD SINK IF IT TOOK TOO LONG TO SECURE PATHS TO THE BEACH.

SOLDIERS CONTINUED DEPLOYMENT AT 140 YARDS FROM THE BEACH...

OUR MISSION IS TO PROTECT THE OMAHA'S RIGHT FLANK. WE'VE GOTTA HEAD TO THE ROAD, BACK THERE, AND SET UP A ROAD BLOCK...

WHERE THIS 20 MILLIMETRE CANNON CAN'T HIT US.

POINTE DU HOC

WHY AT THIS INTERSECTION, LIEUTENANT?

THAT'S WHERE WE'RE GOING TO MEET UP WITH THE 116TH INFANTRY REGIMENT OF THE 29TH DIVISION TO MARCH TOGETHER TO ISIGNY.

LET'S HEAD ON OUT, BOYS!

GOOD. NOW THAT WE'VE ESTABLISHED OUR DEFENSIVE POSITION, WE'VE GOT TO KEEP CONTACT WITH THE ENEMY. WE'VE GOTTA KNOW WHERE HE IS, REMIND HIM THAT WE'RE HERE...

AND KEEP HIM FROM ORGANIZING ANY KIND OF COUNTERATTACK.

JACK, PACO, AND STEVE, FORM PATROLS OF A DOZEN MEN AND GO LEAPFROGGING SOUTH OF THE ROAD!

WE'VE ALSO GOT TO FIGURE OUT WHERE THEY'RE HIDING THOSE FAMOUS CANNONS!

HEY JACK, YOU SEE THOSE TRACKS IN THE FIELD? WEIRD, HUH?

YEAH. LET'S FOLLOW THEM.

3/4

STAFF SERGEANT JACK KUHN AND FIRST SERGEANT LEN LOMELL WERE HARDLY COMFORTED BY WHAT THEY SAW.

MY GOD! HERE ARE THE CANNONS !!

STAND READY. WE ATTACK IN 15 MINUTES.

HO. THE ENEMY !

REINFORCEMENTS WILL ARRIVE IN NO TIME... WE MUST REGAIN CONTROL OF THE ROAD AT ALL COST ! WE HAVE AT LEAST 50 MEN AND THE ELEMENT OF SURPRISE...

THEY AREN'T WATCHING THE CANNONS*. WE'VE GOTTA DESTROY THEM...

OK, BUT WE'VE GOT TO DO IT WITHOUT THEM NOTICING.

WE'VE EACH GOT A THERMITE GRENADE**...

* THE IRONY OF THIS STORY IS THAT THE GERMANS NEVER RECEIVED ORDERS TO USE THE CANNONS. AND YET, THEY WOULD HAVE BEEN ABLE TO FIRE UPON BOTH UTAH AND OMAHA BEACHES FROM POINTE DU HOC. ** THERMITE GRENADES DO NOT EXPLODE. HEATING UP TO TEMPERATURES OF 3000°C, THEY BURN HOT ENOUGH TO MELT METAL.

37

That'll take care of at least two of 'em.

PAW PAW
TATATA

Jack, the Germans are launching their counterattack.

TAK TAK

Hard to shoot a cannon with no sight.

God damn it! Bullets are flying everywhere up at the intersection!

We've got to finish the job. Let's head back to the company and get more thermite grenades.

PAW

PAW

PAW

PAW

PAW

PAW

For their heroic actions, Sergeants Kuhn and Lomell were decorated with the Distinguished Service Cross after the war had ended.

3/6

38

DURING THAT TIME AT OMAHA, THE SITUATION HAD NOT YET IMPROVED. THE LCTS WERE STILL TURNING IN CIRCLES OFF SHORE WHILE THE GIS FOUGHT DESPERATELY TO SURVIVE AGAINST GERMAN GUNFIRE.

JUMP IN THE WATER!

LUCKILY, THESE GIS AND THOSE OF THE SUBSEQUENT WAVES DIDN'T HAVE THE ASSAULT JACKETS* WITH THE DEFECTIVE STRAPS.

CLICK

SURVIVORS CONTINUED TO GATHER ALONG THE EMBANKMENT. WITH MIXED COMPANIES, INEXISTENT COMMUNICATION, SUPPLIES LOST TO THE SEA... HOPELESS CONFUSION WOULD SOON COME CRASHING DOWN UPON THE BEACH. ALL IS LOST!

FACED WITH SUCH A DISASTER, LIEUTENANT GENERAL BRADLEY WAS FORCED TO MAKE A HEARTBREAKING DECISION.

STOP THE DEPLOYMENT OF REINFORCEMENTS.

ABANDON OMAHA?!! WHAT ABOUT OUR BOYS? THEY'LL ALL BE STUCK THERE...

IF WE'RE GOING TO SAVE THIS OPERATION THEN WE DON'T HAVE THE CHOICE.

ORDER ALL PILOTS TO DEPLOY THE REST OF THE TROOPS ON UTAH BEACH. WE'VE TAKEN THE BEACH.

LUCKILY, THREE OTHER GROUPS OF SOLDIERS, FOLLOWING PETER'S EXAMPLE, DECIDED TO ACT RATHER THAN WAIT TO DIE.

THEIR ACTIONS WOULD CHANGE THE COURSE OF THE BATTLE.

* THE DEFECTIVE ASSAULT JACKETS WERE ONLY WORN BY THE FIRST TWO WAVES OF SOLDIERS BECAUSE NOT ENOUGH HAD BEEN MADE.

AT THAT SAME MOMENT, THE NAVAL COMMANDERS, IGNORING DIRECT ORDERS, DECIDED TO MOVE IN CLOSER TO THE BEACHES FOR A MORE PRECISE VIEW OF THEIR OBJECTIVES.

BUT CAPTAIN ?!!! WE'RE PUTTING OURSELVES IN RANGE OF THE GERMAN CANNONS !

I KNOW ! ADVANCE!

HERE AND THERE, CLEVER SOLDIERS CLEAR PATHS FOR THE LANDING CRAFT TO UNLOAD HEAVY MATERIALS...

AT THAT MOMENT, AND AFTER 2 HOURS OF UNRELENTING COMBAT...

WE'RE HOLDING POSITION, SERGEANT.

IGNITE THE RED SMOKE GRENADE.

AT 0900 HOURS, THE GIS HAD PIERCED THE FRONT AT FOUR SPOTS AND HAD TAKEN HOLD OF ONLY ONE GERMAN POSITION.

AT 0930 HOURS, THE MAJOR GENERAL CANCELLED HIS ORDERS TO ABORT DEPLOYMENT AT OMAHA. LUCKILY, THE REDEPLOYMENT OF TROOPS AT UTAH BEACH HAD YET TO COMMENCE.

BY 1030 HOURS, 2 OPENINGS ON THE BEACH HAD BEEN SECURED.

FOR AS MUCH AS HAD HAPPENED, THE BATTLE WASN'T OVER YET. THE LAST GERMAN STRONGHOLDS WOULD ONLY BE TAKEN THE NEXT DAY, FOLLOWING A DAY OF NON-STOP FIGHTING.

IN ALL, OVER 1,200 GIS* GAVE THEIR LIVES FOR VICTORY OF A MISSION THAT DIDN'T GO ACCORDING TO THE MAJOR GENERAL'S

* 1,200 DEAD, 2,682 INJURED

THE CROSSROAD AT POINTE DU HOC.

THEY JUST KEEP COMIN', SARGE. WE JUST LOST ANOTHER THIRTY MEN...

AND WE'RE ALMOST OUT OF AMMO. WE CAN'T HOLD 'EM OFF MUCH LONGER.

I KNOW ALL THAT, GARETH, BUT I DON'T HAVE ANY OTHER IDEA! COMMUNICATIONS ARE DOWN. I CAN'T GET THE SHIP TO SEND REINFORCEMENTS.

WE'RE HOLDIN' ON BY A THREAD AND THE ENEMY JUST KEEPS COMING AND COMING...

THIS MAY BE THE END, BOYS.

THIS REALLY IS THE END, SARGE! THEY LAUNCH ONE MORE ATTACK AND WE'RE GONERS!

PAW PAW

PAW TATATA

TATATATATA

WHA...WHAT A MIRACLE...

BY THE GRACE OF GOD YOU GUYS SHOWED IN THE NICK OF TIME! WHERE DID YOU COME FROM?

WE GOT LOST AROUND OMAHA. I DON'T KNOW HOW WE DID IT! WE MADE IT ACROSS ENEMY LINES AND HERE WE ARE...

ON THE MORNING OF THE 7TH, THE TROOPS FROM OMAHA WERE BARELY ON THE OUTSKIRTS OF VIERVILLE AND THE RANGERS WERE STILL ALL ALONE. THEY HADN'T SLEPT FOR TWO DAYS AND NIGHTS.

COLONEL, THE SHIP HAS FINALLY RECEIVED WORD OF OUR SITUATION. THEY KNOW THAT WE DON'T HAVE ENOUGH MEN TO HOLD THE HOC AND THE ROAD...

THEY'RE ORDERING US TO LEAVE THE FRONT. WE HAVE TO LEAVE THE ROAD AND GO BACK TO SUPPORT DEFENCES ON THE CLIFF.

TELL 'EM THAT WE'VE GOT ALMOST NO AMMO, NO FOOD, AND THAT OUR INJURED ARE IN TERRIBLE CONDITION. *

TELL 'EM TO SEND REINFORCEMENTS! AND FAST!

* BETWEEN THE BATTLE AT POINTE DU HOC AND ALL OF THE COUNTERATTACKS, THE RANGERS MUST HAVE ENGAGED OVER ONE THOUSAND GERMAN SOLDIERS IN COMBAT. OF THE INITIAL 225 RANGERS, ONLY 90 WERE STILL IN CONDITION FOR COMBAT BY NIGHTFALL ON JUNE 8TH.

MARINES FROM THE USS TEXAS LAND AT POINTE DU HOC, BRINGING WITH THEM FOOD AND AMMUNITION.

WHOA! SHOTS ARE STILL FIRING LEFT AND RIGHT UP THERE!

YEAH. IT'S ABOUT TIME WE GOT HERE. OUR BOYS HAVE GOTTA BE IN A SORRY STATE.

TA TA TA TA TA

SOLDIERS TOO INJURED FOR BATTLE BUT STILL CAPABLE OF CLIMBING DOWN THE CLIFF MEET THE LANDING CRAFT.

BY THE EVENING OF JUNE 7TH, THE SECTOR WAS CONSIDERED NEUTRALIZED.

AT THAT MOMENT, THE 3RD BATTALION OF THE 29TH DIVISION'S 116TH INFANTRY REGIMENT, COMING FROM OMAHA, MADE THEIR WAY TOWARD THE RANGERS.

4₁

IN THE CITY OF SAINT PIERRE-DU-MONT, SITUATED LESS THAN ONE KILOMETRE FROM THE RANGERS' COMMAND POST, THE AMERICAN FORCES ADVANCE.

SEEING THE ENEMY COME FROM THIS SIDE AS WELL, THE APPREHENSIVE GERMANS DON'T DARE ATTEMPT A COUNTERATTACK...

WHICH WORKS OUT WELL BECAUSE...

ANOTHER COUNTERATTACK WILL WIPE US OUT. THE MEN ARE BEYOND EXHAUSTION, COLONEL...

ON THE MORNING OF THE 8TH, THE MAJOR GENERAL, STILL AT SEA, PRESUMES THAT THE ATTACK ON THE CLIFF HAD FAILED, ORDERING AN AIR STRIKE...

P 47 PILOTS WERE READY TO RAIN HELLFIRE UPON THE RANGERS WHEN...

HEY, FELLAS! THEY'RE OURS! THEY'RE GONNA BOMB US!!

ABORT MISSION! ALL PILOTS, REPEAT : ABORT MISSION. OUR MEN HAVE THE CLIFF! ABORT MISSION..

42

44

TA TA TA TA TA TA TA TA

WHAT A RELIEF! NOW THAT THEY KNOW THAT WE'VE GOT THE CLIFF... THEY'LL FINALLY SEND US REINFORCEMENTS...

NOT ANY TOO SOON, EITHER! THREE DAYS AND NIGHTS WITH- OUT SLEEP... I'M DEAD TIRED!

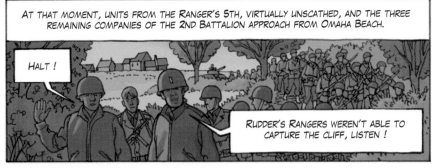

AT THAT MOMENT, UNITS FROM THE RANGER'S 5TH, VIRTUALLY UNSCATHED, AND THE THREE REMAINING COMPANIES OF THE 2ND BATTALION APPROACH FROM OMAHA BEACH.

HALT !

RUDDER'S RANGERS WEREN'T ABLE TO CAPTURE THE CLIFF, LISTEN !

LISTEN TO WHAT, CAPTAIN ?

OUR MACHINE GUNS SHOOT BETWEEN 400 AND 600 ROUNDS A MINUTE. GERMAN GUNS ARE BETWEEN 1,200 AND 1,500. THOSE SHOTS WERE FIRED FROM A GERMAN WEAPON...

HEAD ON OUT! WE'VE GOT ANOTHER FIGHT AHEAD OF US.

PAW PAW PAW

AAAH!

WHAT THE DEVIL!!

HEY!! THOSE AREN'T GERMANS WE'RE SHOOTING AT, CAPTAIN! THOSE ARE RANGERS!!!

HOLD YOUR FIRE!

THOUGHT YOU BOYS DIDN'T MAKE IT...

EVERYBODY THOUGHT THAT. EVEN ON BOARD THE U.S.S TEXAS THEY THOUGHT THAT. YOU KILLED TWO OF MY MEN AND INJURED 6 OTHERS, CAPTAIN...

YES, IT'S HORRIBLE !

43

AND WHEN I FOUND OUT THAT ONE OF THE COLONELS WAS COMING TO THE POINTE DU HOC, I DIDN'T HESITATE A SECOND. NOT KNOWING WHETHER YOU MADE IT OR NOT WAS TOO PAINFUL.

WE BOTH MADE IT, BROTHER. AND FOR YOU THE WAR IS OVER!

I'M NOT GOING BACK JIM. I CAN'T!

I GUESS YOU'RE HEADED BACK HOME TOMORROW? WHEN YOU GET BACK, THE PAPERS ARE GOING TO GO CRAZY FOR YOUR SKETCHES.

YOU MADE IT, BRO. YOU'RE GOING TO BE A HUGE STAR!

WHAT ?!!!

THE FOLKS, GLENDA... EVERYBODY'LL BE WAITING FOR GOOD OL' PETER TO COME HOME.

HE DOESN'T EXIST ANYMORE !

PETER, IF YOU WANT TO REJOIN THE BIG RED ONE, IT'S NOW OR NEVER!

PETER... NO! WAIT !!!

TAKE CARE OF YOURSELF, BROTHER.

JIM !

PETER !

46

HEY, GUYS!! ... MY BROTHER JUMPED ON A MINE!!! OVER HERE! HURRY! YOU GOTTA SAVE HIM!!

SORRY, SOLDIER! DON'T HAVE THE TIME! WE'VE ALREADY GOT PLENTY OF WORK!!

HANG IN THERE, JIM! I KNOW AN ENGLISH DOCTOR! I'M GONNA CALL HIM! IT'S GONNA BE OK, JIM! EVERYTHING'S GONNA BE JUST FINE!!

ROGUE TO 30TH BRITISH CORPS, ROGUE TO 30TH BRITISH CORPS, OVER.

ROGUE, 30TH BRITISH CORPS HERE. WHAT'S YOUR REQUEST? OVER.

45

47

THE END

46

48

NORMANDY

JUNE 44

a dossier from Isabelle BOURNIER and Marc POTTIER

Soldiers, Sailors and Airmen of the Allied Expeditionary Force!

You are about to embark upon the Great Crusade, toward which we have striven these many months. The eyes of the world are upon you. The hopes and prayers of liberty-loving people everywhere march with you. In company with our brave Allies and brothers-in-arms on other Fronts, you will bring about the destruction of the German war machine, the elimination of Nazi tyranny over the oppressed peoples of Europe, and security for ourselves in a free world. [...] I have full confidence in your courage and devotion to duty and skill in battle. We will accept nothing less than full Victory!

Good luck! And let us beseech the blessing of Almighty God upon this great and noble undertaking.

The D-Day Statement from General Dwight D. Eisenhower, Supreme Commander of the Allied Expeditionary Force, distributed to all the members of the expeditionary force on the eve of the invasion.

OPERATION *Overlord*

It was at the Casablanca Conference, in January 1943, when Roosevelt and Churchill made the decision to attack the Reich by launching a vast landing operation on the European continent. The Combined Chiefs of Staff created COSSAC, an Anglo-American planning staff of thousands of strategists, to plan one of the largest military operations of the 20th Century.

Why Normandy?

The Combined Chiefs of Staff needed first to determine an assault sector. While the Pas de Calais, with its proximity to Great Britain, seemed like a favourable landing site, the coastal defences of the Atlantic Wall were far too strong. The coast of Normandy, however, presented different advantages: long, sandy beaches shielded from strong winds by the Cotentin peninsula, deep-water ports like that of Cherbourg to the West and Le Havre to the East, a coast with lightly-fortified defences, and the possibility to cut off the coastal highway to prevent any German reinforcements from a counterattack. After much deliberation, it was decided in July of 1943 that the landings would take place on the 1st of May, 1944, in the Bay of the Seine, on three beaches: two British and one American (the future Omaha being code named Beach 313). In early 1944, Eisenhower and Montgomery decided to expand the landing to five beaches. Requiring additional preparations, the launching of the bridgehead would be delayed by one month from the original landing date.

Aerial bombardments were launched to cut off enemy lines of communication.

Officers from the 6th British Airborne Division synchronize their watches before taking off for Normandy.

Anchored at a distance, Naval artillery fires at the defences of the Atlantic Wall.

The Three Phases of the Landings

D-Day can be broken down into three main operations: airborne landings, aerial bombings, and the naval assault with soldiers landing on the beaches.

During the night of June 5th and 6th, paratroops landed at the two extremities of the landing zone, marking the beginning of Operation Overlord. Their mission: Protect and facilitate the assault on the beaches and cut any line of communication to prevent a German counteroffensive.

To the East, in the Ranville-Bénouville sector, General Gale and his 6th Airborne Division had the objective of gaining control of the Merville Battery while to the west, in the Sainte-Mère-Eglise sector, the American 82nd and 101st Airborne Divisions received orders to take control of roads and bridges with access to the landing beaches.

The paratrooper operations, crucial for the success of the June 6th landings, unfortunately concluded with tremendous losses.

Beginning in April of 1944,

bombardments of the Atlantic Wall batteries by the RAF and the US Air Force continue up to the night of the 5th and 6th. Despite the thousands of tons of bombs dropped on enemy defences, the effectiveness of the bombardments were varying. At the dawn of June 6th, the Naval artillery took over and, for 30 minutes, fiercely attacked without managing to silence the German coastal artillery definitively.

With the bombings terminated,

the third phase of the military operation could commence. Packed with soldiers and material, the landing crafts took to the water and headed toward the beaches. Because of the tides, there was a time-delay on the assault of the five beaches, starting with Utah (to the West) and ending with Sword (to the East).

The assault on the beaches took place in successive waves. Here, the second wave approaches Omaha Beach. It is 0700 hours.

Operation Fortitude

To divert the enemy's attention toward other decoy operations, the Allied Command put into place Operation Fortitude, which consisted of making the Germans believe that the landings would take place either in Norway (Fortitude North), or in the Pas de Calais (Fortitude South). The Allies created fake airfields in the south of England and named General Patton Commander–in–chief of a fictitious army equipped with inflatable tanks and plywood vehicles. This colossal and intricately deceptive operation would become one of the keys to the success of the landings.

TIMING, THE MEN
and the location of the Landings

The assault on the beaches of Normandy is considered one of the most important operations of the 20th Century. Its success came not from a miracle, but rather from the lessons learned from earlier landings, including specific materials needed and an effective deployment strategy for the landing craft. Overlord was also, and perhaps above all, a matter of men with the audacity to undertake this monumental operation.

MAY 8TH, 1944, IN LONDON. GENERAL MONTGOMERY REPORTED THAT THE ALLIED TROOPS HAD REACHED THEIR HEIGHT OF READINESS. IT WAS TIME TO SET THE DATE FOR THE LANDING OPERATION. THEY CHOSE THE 5TH OF JUNE AT DAWN.

The Timing
1942
August 19th: *Allied raid on the beach at Dieppe*

Allied raid on the beach at Dieppe, August 19th, 1942. This first attempt at a landing ends in failure.

November 8th: *Allied landings in North Africa*

Landing in Sicily in July 1943. The Allies will soon launch a naval operation on Italy.

1943
January 24th: *Casablanca Conference: the decision is made to land in Europe.*
July 10th: *Allied landing in Sicily*
September 8-9th: Landing in Salerno, Italy

1944
January 22nd: *Landings in Anzio, Italy*
February: *Revision of Operation Overlord and expansion of the sector to five beaches*
Mid-May: Eisenhower sets a date of June 5th for the Normandy landing
June 3rd: *Troops launched for Normandy*
June 6th: *Normandy landing*
0020 hours: 6th Airborne Division lands at Ranville
0030 hours: 101st Airborne Division

ON MAY 15TH, BEFORE THE KING OF ENGLAND AND SIR WINSTON CHURCHILL, AIR MARSHAL A.W. TEDDER PRESENTED THE FINAL PLANS TO THE ALLIED HIGH COMMAND. THE LANDING WOULD TAKE PLACE IN NORMANDY BETWEEN THE MOUTH OF THE RIVER ORNE AND CARENTAN BAY.

US TROOPS WILL LAND ON UTAH AND OMAHA WHILE BRITISH AND CANADIAN FORCES WILL LAND ON GOLD, JUNO, AND SWORD BEACHES.

IN PREPARATION, AIRBORNE FORCES WILL PARACHUTE TO THE WEST OF CARENTAN BAY AND TO THE EAST OF THE ORNE.

lands at Sainte-Mère-Eglise
0630 hours: Landings on Omaha Beach and Utah Beach
0710 hours: Soldiers land at the foot of the cliff at Pointe du Hoc
0730 hours: Landings on Gold Beach and Sword Beach
0800 hours: Landing on Juno Beach
June 7th: *Beginning of construction of the artificial ports at Omaha and Arromanches*
June 19-22nd: *Storm destroys artificial port at Omaha*
June 27th: *Capture of the port of Cherbourg*
July 8th and 19th: *Liberation of Caen*
August 15th: *Allied landing in Provence*
August 21st: *End of the Battle of Normandy*
August 25th: *Liberation of Paris*

1945
May 8th: *End of the war in Europe*
September 2nd: *End of the war in the Pacific*

The Men

For the Allies:
General Dwight David Eisenhower (1890-1969)

Eisenhower was 54 at the time of the Normandy Landings. Having already been in charge of landings in North Africa in 1942 and Italy in 1943, he was named Supreme Commander of the Allied Forces; merited not only for his organizational skills, but also for his indispensable diplomatic qualities exhibited while leading a multinational army and arbitrating the misunderstandings between its generals. With a career already out of the ordinary, he would be elected President of the United States in 1952.

SHAEF (Supreme Headquarters Allied Expeditionary Force), February of 1944. From left to right: General Bradley, Admiral Ramsay, Air Chief Marshal Tedder, General Eisenhower, General Montgomery, Air Marshal Leigh-Mallory, and General Bedell-Smith.

General Bernard Law Montgomery (1887-1976)

Having become well-known after bringing victory against Field Marshal Rommel at El-Alamein, in North Africa, General Montgomery, nicknamed Monty, was also known for his difficult character and his strong spirit of independence. In January of 1944, he was named Ground Forces Commander and had the mission of planning the Normandy Landings. He quickly decided to expand the assault by adding two more beaches: Utah and Sword.

For the Germans:
Field Marshal Erwin Rommel (1891-1944)

Known as "Desert Fox" for his tactical abilities demonstrated in North Africa, Rommel was considered the most famous officer of the Wehrmacht. Ambitious and favoured by Hitler, he was named Commander-in-Chief of Army B, positioned in Normandy. Rommel received orders to accelerate construction of the Atlantic Wall and to handle the counterattack in case of invasion.

Field Marshal Gerd von Rundstedt (1875-1953)

At 68, von Rundstedt was the eldest German officer. Hitler named him Commander-in-Chief on the western front and placed him under the orders of Field Marshal Rommel. The two men hardly got along and were in utter discord regarding

Field Marshal von Rundstedt (left) and Field Marshal Rommel (right) strongly differ regarding the strategy to adopt in case of invasion.

the strategy to adopt in case of invasion. Rundstedt defended the idea that it was necessary to allow the assailants to invade before organizing a counterattack, while Rommel, in opposition, declared that they had to force the Allies back to sea within the first hours of an attack.

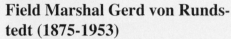

Dossier:

NORMANDY *JUNE 44*

OMAHA *bloody Omaha*

In the American sector, the landing was set for 0630 hours or one hour before the beginning of the rising tide. At Omaha, the troops' objective was to establish a solid bridgehead and then to advance toward the south, in the direction of Saint-Lô, all the while establishing a link with the adjacent beaches: Utah and Gold.

> ## American Troops
> 5th Army Corps (General Gerow)
> of the 1st US Army (General Bradley)
> 1st Division "The Big Red One" (General Huebner)
> 29th Division "Twenty-Nine Let's Go" (General Gerhardt)
> 1st company of the 2nd battalion of the Rangers (Pointe de la Percée)
> General Gerow commanded 35,000 soldiers.

Omaha Beach: 0630 Hours

In the early hours, tossed about by the heavy swell, the landing craft make their way through the obstacles that explode at contact. The amphibious tanks, put into the water to protect soldiers from enemy fire, are unable to resist the assault of the crashing waves. Only five of them would reach the shore.

Waiting until the men set foot on land before going into action, the German machine guns suddenly open fire on the GIs who desperately search for cover on the beach.

A Well-guarded Beach

Situated atop of the steep cliffs surrounding Omaha beach, the German defences dominated the open sea, denying all assailants to land and to take to the small valleys leading inland. The beach itself was riddled with obstacles: posts, ramps, and barriers... Some were topped with mines, while others were equipped with metal spikes to tear open landing craft.

Field Marshal Rommel and his staff inspect the defences of the Atlantic Wall.

The 716th Infantry Division, commanded by General Richter, had been instructed to defend this sector. Consisting of young recruits, older soldiers, and two battalions of Georgians, this division counted for 8,000 mediocre soldiers. Three months before D-Day, they received reinforcements from the mobile and well-equipped 352nd ID, battle-hardened by combat on the Eastern Front.

THREE DAYS BEFORE D-DAY, THE 3RD REGIMENT, COMPOSED OF EXPERIENCED SOLDIERS RETURNING FROM THE EASTERN FRONT, JOINED THE FORCES ALREADY GUARDING THE COAST.

Loaded with heavy equipment, the infantrymen attempt to take to the shore.

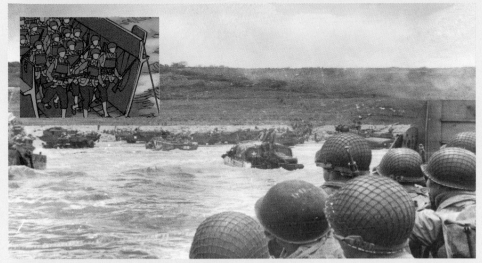

Amphibious trucks and landing craft head for the shoreline in successive waves.

The first aide received. The injured were evacuated to Great Britain by boat.

On the beach, soldiers run for cover. There is nothing to shelter them from enemy fire.

"There are two kinds of men on this beach: the dead, and those about to die." Colonel Taylor

Once on land, the operation turns to total chaos, with the 16th and 116th regiments continuing to arrive in successive waves. It is urgent that pathways be cleared to navigate through the obstacles. Moreover, the exits from the beach have to be taken so that troops and vehicles can advance inland.

At 0800 hours, it is a catastrophe! Out of the surviving officers, Colonel Taylor (16th IR) convinces his men to make a last ditch effort to get off of the beach. Exhausted, the soldiers manage to get over the dunes. Meanwhile, two destroyers at sea take a risk; advancing to less than one kilometre away from the coast, they succeed in taking out German defences.

Around 0900 hours, Bradley, aboard the USS Augusta, sends a message to Eisenhower requesting permission to abort the operation. Luckily, Ike did not receive it until later in the afternoon. The soldiers who had been under attack had managed to get off of the beach.

ID: Infantry Division
IR: Infantry Regiment
DUKW: amphibious truck
LCT: Landing Craft Tank

Omaha Beach: D-Day Losses at 50%

Bad weather conditions and human errors were responsible for the enormous difficulties that this operation encountered. Overtaken by five-foot tall waves, the amphibious tanks filled with water and then sank. The same situation was true for the DUKWs transporting artillery. The heavy swell strongly impaired in the firing of the LCTs which intended to destroy German defences just before the soldiers took to the ground. The US Air Force was also unsuccessful with its bombings. Flying blind because of the clouds, and using a weak calibre, the bombardments left the coastal artillery nearly untouched. In all, the little time allotted to the naval artillery to neutralizing the German cannons, the distance from the shore of the landing craft drop-off points, and the presence of the 352nd German Infantry Division resulted in the disorganization of the landing at Omaha.

US RANGERS

The Assault on the Pointe du Hoc

At the summit of Pointe du Hoc, a German artillery battery was supposedly harbouring six powerful long range cannons, which would make the entire landing operation impossible on Utah and Omaha beaches. The destruction of this dangerous enemy post would be the mission entrusted to Colonel Rudder and his 2nd battalion of Rangers. To successfully complete their mission, they would have to land at the foot of the cliff on either side of the point and climb the sheer cliff face. Once atop the cliff, they were to neutralize the cannons and advance inland to obstruct any German reinforcements headed for Omaha.

Rock Solid Training...

As soon as he was informed of his mission, Rudder began training his men on the cliffs of the Isle of Wight. There, they ran training exercises along with putting together specialized equipment: a rocket propelled knotted cords or rope ladders attached to grappling hooks, booster rockets that unravelled small ropes, extension ladders, etc. To complete their preparation for the mission, the Rangers studied aerial reconnaissance photos as well as small scale models of the terrain.

Bombardiers from the 9th US Air Force, dropping bombs on German fortified positions.

The Landing Fleet Adrift!

On the night of June 5th and 6th, the US Air Force caused heavy damage on top of the cliff. The platforms supporting the cannons were destroyed and the ground had been pounded by the shells. Around 0430 hours, landing craft and amphibious trucks, loaded with soldiers and material, took to sea. Arrival at the cliff base was scheduled for 0630 hours, the same time that the Naval artillery would cease-fire.

Unfortunately, following a navigational error caused by strong coastal currents and thick

fog, the 225 Rangers drifted toward the Pointe de la Percée. Colonel Rudder's fleet had no choice ; they would have to turn around and run alongside the cliff under enemy fire to reach their primary objective. Taking advantage of these wasted 40 minutes, the defenders would have the time to organise their counterattack.

Colonel James E. Rudder, commander of the 2nd battalion of Rangers.

On the rocky beach, the men prepare to scale the cliff while rope ladders are fixed to the rock face by grapples fired from rocket launchers on the landing craft.

The Assault on the Cliff

At 0710 hours, the Rangers finally arrive at the foot of the cliff. The assault on the cliff will take place on only one side due to a loss of men and materials. Thirty metres overhead, machine guns rip into action while, at sea, two destroyers answer their fire. Using the rockfall caused by the Naval artillery, the assailants heaved themselves all the way up the cliff face by ropes fixed to grappling hooks at the summit. At 0730 hours, 150 able-bodied men reached the top of the point and pushed the German defenders back into their bunkers. Despite their great feat, a great disappointment awaits : there are no cannons!

Two Days of Fierce Combat

While in the middle of heavy combat, the stupefied Rangers discover that the German stronghold is devoid of cannons. While one part of the troops continues the combat atop the point, another heads inland in search of the missing artillery which they end up finding near an empty dirt road, about one kilometre from the coast. The cannons had been moved to shelter during the air assaults and replaced with camouflaged beams to deceive the Resistance and any study of aerial photos.

After putting them out of

commission, the Rangers, impatiently awaiting reinforcements landing at Omaha, find themselves face to face with a German counterattack coming from Isigny.

Reinforcements finally arrive! Like their fellow soldiers from the first assault wave, the Rangers regroup at the foot of the cliff.

Atop the cliff at Pointe du Hoc, the German defenders, taking up position in the bunkers, would hold out against the American soldiers until the morning of June 8th. It is thanks to the destroyers' fire that Rudder would finally succeed in taking the point; a military feat that will forever rest etched in the memory of the Normandy Landings.

Of the 225 Rangers involved in the assault, only 90 remain fit for combat.

DD TANKS,
Funnies and Other Inventions

Following the failure of the attempted landing at Dieppe in August, 1942, due in large part to the absence of ground support for the assault waves, Allied strategists developed equipment theoretically appropriate for the terrains and conditions of June 6th. Sometimes effective, other times completely impractical, these inventions also shed light on the story behind the longest day.

Beached Crab Tank

DD Tanks and General Hobart's Funnies

Under the direction of Major-General Percy Hobart, General Montgomery's brother-in-law, Churchill tanks and Sherman tanks were designed and modified to adapt to specific missions without compromising their firepower. For example, the Crab tank was equipped with a rotating flail for exploding mines in its path. The Crocodile tank was equipped with a flame-thrower. The Bobbin deployed its reel of steel-reinforced canvas on the soft sand of the beaches, permitting other vehicles to pass without sinking. All of these curious creations were nicknamed Hobart's Funnies. The most astonishing, however, was surely the DD tank. Named after its double drive, the Duplex Drive tank was a Sherman M4 equipped with

a flotation screen, theoretically allowing it to float. Launched at high sea, the DD tanks were supposed to reach the beaches at the same time as the first assault wave, providing ground support for the troops. Unfortunately at Omaha, the DD tanks were launched too far from the shore and in rough waters, sinking nearly every one of them along with their equipment. The absence of this firepower was a large factor in the

DD Tank with flotation screen

self-sacrifice. But after 48 hours of combat, only 90 Rangers were still in combat condition, Colonel Rudder having been injured twice.

WE'RE SLIDING!

CAN'T CLIMB OVER THESE ROCKS.

American casualties at "Bloody Omaha."

"The ramp was again lowered, and the first tank was launched. The water was much deeper than expected, and as the tank went off the ramp it went to the bottom and settled. The tank commander gave the order to abandon tank and the entire crew was brought back to the ship by means of a heaving line thrown from the LCT."
Ensign F.S. White

Scaling the Pointe du Hoc

At the head of these Rangers from Texas, the courageous, 34 year-old Colonel Rudder, along with his 225 men, has to scale the shear cliffside of the Pointe du Hoc. To aide in climbing this obstacle, the Rangers fire their special rocket launchers, equipped with grap-ples and rope, transported in the landing craft. Soaked and heavy, the ropes fall short of the cliff top. Long firemen's ladders are also used to reach the top. The German defenders, as in the days of castle sieges, try to push back the ladders. A lone DUKW (amphibious truck), equipped with a 33 metres long ladder and topped with a double machine gun lands near the cliff. The gunman, Sergeant William Stivison, fires like a metronome, providing cover for the Rangers; but the ground is unstable and forces him to cease fire. The Rangers would capture Pointe du Hoc thanks to their military means, both modern and archaic, as well as their courage and

At 0600 hours on D-Day, Colonel James E. Rudder said to his men, "Listen up Rangers! Show them what you're made of... Good luck, men! Destroy them... Departure in five minutes."

11

THE REPORTERS
of June 6th

Informing the masses about the war was one of the Allies top priorities; so many war reporters found themselves in the middle of the assault on the beaches of Normandy. Under enemy fire and with fear in their bellies, photographers, cameramen, and other official painters were the first witnesses of D-Day. The knowledge and memory of this day, the longest day, is due in great part to the legacy of their work.

Manuel Bromberg shows medics caring for the injured at Omaha.

"If Your Pictures Aren't Good Enough, You're Not Close Enough." *Robert Capa*

"The next mortar shell fell between the barbed wire and the sea, and every piece of shrapnel found a man's body. The Irish priest and the Jewish doctor were the first to stand up on the «Easy Red» beach. I shot the picture. The next shell fell even closer. I didn't dare to take my eyes off the finder of my Contax and frantically shot frame after frame. Half a minute later, my camera jammed— my roll was finished. I reached in my bag for a new roll,

"The War at the Tip of a Charcoal Pencil"

With a gun in one hand, khaki sketchpad in the other, and a Leica camera strapped around his neck, the official painter of the American Army, Manuel Bromberg, was a real-life Peter MacTavish from the comic. Enlisted in 1942 and integrated into the US War Art Unit one year later, Bromberg landed on Omaha. 18 artists made up this select unit, 3 of which being assigned to each of the theatres of war. Bromberg's sketches do not depict heroic battles; his voluntary

use of vague lines suggests violence and suffering.

and my wet, shaking hands ruined the roll before I could insert it in my camera. I paused for a moment . . . and then I had it bad. The empty camera trembled in my hands. It was a new kind of fear shaking my body from head to toe, and twisting my face. I unhooked my shovel and

tried to dig a hole. The shovel hit stone under the sand and I hurled it away. The men around me lay motionless. Only the dead on the waterline rolled with the waves."

Robert Capa, Slightly Out of Focus, Modern Library, 1999

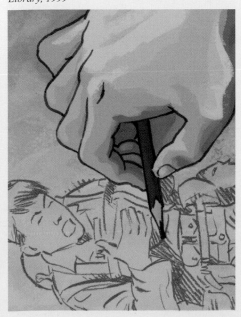

In 1944, Robert Capa was 31 years old. Already a famous photographer after his coverage of the Spanish Civil War, he was a Life Magazine correspondent. At Omaha Beach, with 3 cameras, a Rolleiflex and two Contax, he took part in the first assault wave. In the middle of hell, he would finish all of his rolls of film. Holding his cameras out of the water, high above his head, Capa caught a small boat back to deliver his precious photos as quickly as possible to Life. Unfortunately, during development, only 11 photos of the 72 taken were saved, and those were still out of focus. The editor at Life dared to say that Capa's hands were shaking. In response to these accusations, Capa entitled his war memoirs "Slightly Out of Focus."

"Everybody could see that something had gone wrong" John MacVane

Landing with the first assault wave, the 1st US Army had 13 journalists and war correspondents. All of the big American media at the time, New York Herald Tribune, Chicago Tribune, Los Angeles Times... sent a special correspondent; among them, John MacVane of Radio NBC. Unfortunately for him, all of the radio transmitters

fell in the water. He had to wait until the next day, Wednesday, June 7th, around one o'clock in the morning, before he found the proper equipment to transmit for only 15 minutes. Regrettably, no one would be able to pick up his signal.

THE AMERICAN LEGACY
of June 6th

For the Americans, the 6th of June, 1944, remains a time in history where Good defeated Evil. The sacrifice of American soldiers at Omaha Beach and at the Pointe du Hoc is forever etched in history as the archetype of a just war where democracy and human rights triumph over barbarity and Nazism. The memory of the places, the commemorative ceremonies and the cinematographic productions of Hollywood will ensure forever the memory of the grandeur, the courage, and the self-sacrifice of the American people for the liberation of Europe.

The American Cemetery at Colleville

On nearly 70 hectares of land perpetually conceded to the United States from France, the American Cemetery at Colleville is situated atop the cliff overlooking Omaha Beach. The American Battle Monuments Commission is in charge of the care and upkeep of this cemetery where every year nearly 1.5 million visitors come to pay their respects to the graves of 9,386 interred Americans of which 307 are unknown soldiers.

In reading the inscriptions engraved on the crosses, you can find a father and son buried side by side, as well as the 33 cases of two brothers, and also Theodore Roosevelt Junior, oldest son of former President Theodore Roosevelt.

The rows of white crosses at the American Cemetery at Colleville-sur-Mer reinforce the grandeur and majesty of the location.

The Memorial, situated on the edge of the cemetery, is composed of a semicircular colonnade with a loggia at each end. Positioned in the middle, a bronze statue symbolizing the spirit of the American youth sacrificed to bring freedom to the world. Behind the monument, inscribed in the wall of disappeared, you can read the names of 1,557 soldiers who disappeared in the region of which the bodies were never found or formally identified.

From the Memorial, you can access the panoramic view points overlooking the beach, where it is easy to understand, while gazing upon the vast sea, how greatly the terrain favoured the German defenders and why Omaha was the bloodiest sector of the invasion. Each acting president of the United States comes to Colleville du-

ring the large June 6th anniversary ceremonies (the 40th, 50th, or 60th anniversary), where the commemorations at this site carry special symbolism among the grandeur and majesty of the cemetery.

"Liberty road, stone markers strech from Normandy to Bastogne, Belgium, along the route of the liberating American Army"

Saving the Pointe du Hoc

The Pointe du Hoc remains one of the most famous places of the Battle of Normandy. In this memorial, also entrusted to the American Battle Monuments Commission, everything was left untouched, just as it was following combat. Bomb craters and shrapnel, eviscerated bunkers and barbed wire attest to the barrage of gunfire and the violent combat. Walking about this lunar terrain atop the cliff that

Colonel Rudder's men climbed allow to better understand the heroic feat of the Rangers.

But nature and the waves erode the cliff. In only sixty years, the Pointe du Hoc had receded nearly 10 metres. The German command post is threatened with collapsing. Is it imaginable to watch such a historical place progressively disappear?

American and French authorities decided to react. Experts from the University of Texas, the university where Colonel Rudder became president after the war, studied the situation and proposed pouring concrete in the cavities at the foot of the cliff to prevent erosion. The cost would be rather expensive, but it is necessary to save such a symbolic site of American combat.

R. de Lue's statue was erected in honor of the glory of the American youth.

The Pointe du Hoc's ground was cratered and demolished by the intensity of the combat.

15

D-DAY
Books, Films, and Music

For viewing pleasure…

Apocalypse, Henri de Turenne, Louis Costelle, Jean-Louis Guillaud, 2009 (documentary of HD color images).

D-Day in colour, 2004.

Jour J – Battle of Normandy, 2004 (documentary).

Saving Private Ryan, Steven Spielberg, 1998 (fiction).

The Big Red one, Samuel Fuller, 1980 (fiction).

The longest Day, Andrew Marton, 1962 (fiction).

For listening pleasure…

Victory Concert – Echoes of 1944, Claude Bolling big band.

The Essential Glenn Miller (3 CD), Glenn Miller orchestra.

Complete prestige Carnegie Hall 1943-1944, Duke Ellington.

D-Day and the battle of Normandy 1944 by Various artists.

Thanks to Rémy Desquesnes, historian, for his proofreading and advice.

For Reading Pleasure…

Ambrose, Stephen E. : D-Day June 6, 1944 : the battle for the Normandy Beaches, Paperback, 2002.

Ambrose, Stephen E. : Band of Brothers, Paperback, 2001.

Bevor, Antony : D-Day : from the beaches to Paris, Hardcover, 2009.

Desquesnes, Rémy : Normandy 44, Rennes, Ouest-France, 2009.

Holmes, Richard : The D-day experience from invasion to liberation, Hardcover, 2004)

Whelan, Richard and Robert Capa : Robert Capa, the definitive collection, Phaidon Press, 2004.

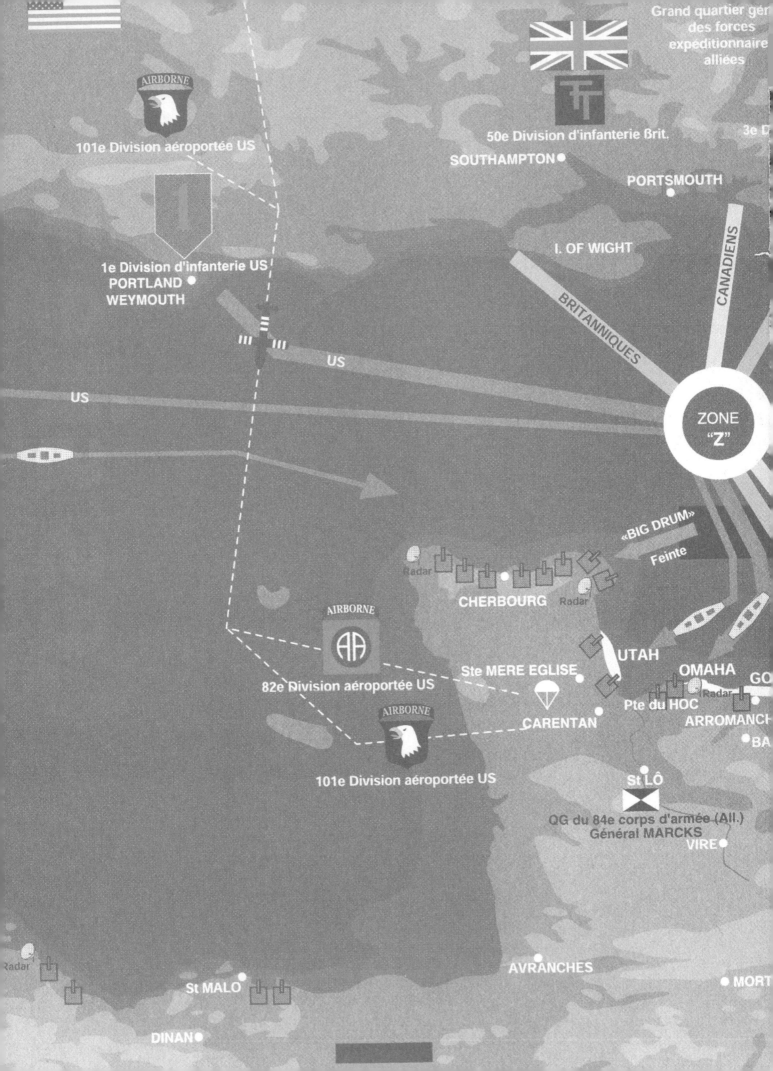